**GEO**

7-17
Lexile: _____
AR/BL: ___5.5_____
AR Points: ___0.5_____

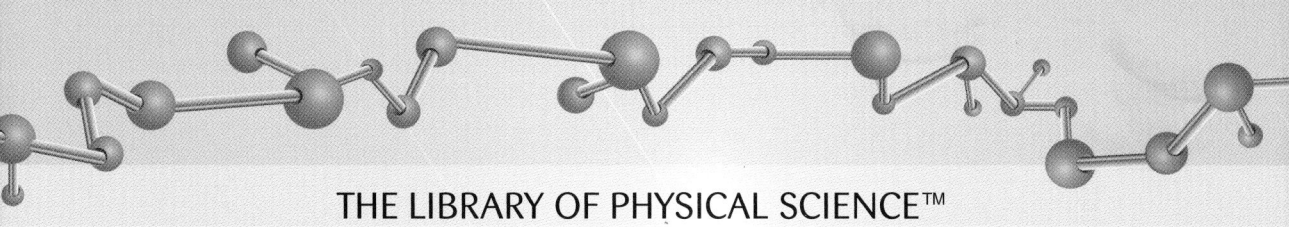

THE LIBRARY OF PHYSICAL SCIENCE™

# The Properties of Liquids

Marylou Morano Kjelle

The Rosen Publishing Group's
PowerKids Press™
New York

*This book is dedicated to my parents, Viola and Frank Morano*

Published in 2007 by The Rosen Publishing Group, Inc.
29 East 21st Street, New York, NY 10010

First Edition

Editors: Daryl Heller, Joanne Randolph, and Suzanne Slade
Book Design: Elana Davidian
Book Layout: Ginny Chu
Photo Researcher: Marty Levick

Photo Credits: Cover, p. 5 © Artville; p. 4 © Kenneth Eward/Biografx/Photo Researchers, Inc.; pp. 6, 12 © Royalty-Free/Corbis; p. 7 © David Young-Wolff/PhotoEdit; pp. 8, 10 © Clive Freeman/BioSym Technologies/Photo Researchers, Inc.; p. 9 © Ralph A. Clevenger/Corbis; p. 11 © Erich Schrempp/Photo Researchers, Inc.; p. 13 © Julie Habel/Corbis; p. 14 © Andrew Lambert Photography/Science Photo Library/Photo Researchers, Inc.; p. 15 © Art Wolfe/Getty Images; p. 16 (left) Cindy Reiman for The Rosen Publishing Group; p. 16 (right) © Digital Stock; p. 17 © Matthew Klein/Corbis; p. 18 © Dirk Wiersma/Science Photo Library/Photo Researchers, Inc.; p. 19 Nature's Images/Photo Researchers, Inc.; p. 20 © Felicia Martinez/PhotoEdit; p. 21 © Nancy P. Alexander/Photo Edit.

Library of Congress Cataloging-in-Publication Data

Kjelle, Marylou Morano.
    The properties of liquids / Marylou Morano Kjelle.— 1st ed.
        p. cm. — (Library of physical science)
    Includes index.
    ISBN 1-4042-3422-5 (library binding) — ISBN 1-4042-2169-7 (pbk.)
    1. Liquids—Juvenile literature. 2. Matter—Properties—Juvenile literature. I. Title. II. Series.
    QC145.24.K54 2007
    530.4'2–dc22
                                                    2005026702

Manufactured in the United States of America

# Contents

Liquid Is One State of Matter     4

Liquids and Volume     6

Liquids and Cold     8

Liquids and Heat     10

Evaporation     12

Condensation     14

Liquids in Solutions     16

Special Properties of Liquids     18

Liquids and Density     20

The Most Important Liquid     22

Glossary     23

Index     24

Web Sites     24

# Liquid Is One State of Matter

Everything in our world is made of matter. Your house, the food you eat, and even your dog are matter. Matter is usually found in three forms, or states. The three states of matter are gas, liquid, and solid.

All matter is made of tiny parts called **atoms**. Atoms are so small you cannot see them. Atoms join with other atoms to form larger parts called molecules. Millions of molecules connect with each other to form every kind of matter.

The molecules that make up solids, liquids, and gases are always moving.

This model of water molecules was made on a computer. It shows how each water molecule includes two hydrogen atoms and one oxygen atom.

Forces of **attraction** between the molecules keep the molecules together. These forces are called intermolecular forces, or bonds. The bonds between molecules in a liquid are weaker than those in a solid but stronger than those in gases. Different liquids have certain properties, or characteristics, that allow us to classify them as liquids. What are some things that seawater, soup, or chocolate milk have in common?

One property of water molecules is that they stick together in drops. These drops can join to form puddles or oceans.

# Liquids and Volume

A liquid has no shape of its own. Instead it takes the shape of the object holding it. For example, if you poured milk from a tall glass into a short mug, the milk would take on the shape of its new **container**.

The amount of space a liquid fills is called its volume. Although a liquid changes shape to fit its container, its volume remains the same. The volume of the milk in the mug is the same as the volume of the milk in the tall glass.

Honey is a thick liquid with strong bonds between its molecules. A liquid's strong intermolecular bonds hold the molecules together and cause its volume to stay the same. The liquid cannot grow larger or become smaller.

Liquids are also able to flow. How fast a liquid flows depends on the strength of its intermolecular bonds. For example, honey is a liquid that flows very slowly. It would take a lot longer to fill a cup with honey than it would to fill the same size cup with water. The bonds that hold the molecules together in honey are stronger than those in water.

Scientists do experiments to see if their beliefs are correct. This girl is proving the scientific fact that a liquid will take the shape of its container.

# Liquids and Cold

Rain may leave puddles of water on the sidewalk. If the air **temperature** drops, the water may turn to ice. Lowering the temperature of a liquid makes the molecules slow down and move closer together. In time the liquid changes into a solid. This is called freezing.

The temperature at which a liquid becomes a solid is its freezing point. At this same temperature, a solid also melts and returns to the liquid state. The freezing point and the melting point of a **substance** are the same temperature. When most liquids freeze, they contract,

When water molecules freeze, like the ones modeled here, they move closer together.

or become smaller and take up less space. Water, however, takes up more space after it freezes. Now that you know this, what do you think would happen if you filled up an ice cube tray to the top with water?

An iceberg is a large floating mass of frozen water. Much of an iceberg is under the water.

# Liquids and Heat

Sometimes heat can change a liquid into a gas. When a liquid is heated, its molecules take in **energy** from the heat and begin to move faster. The warmer the liquid becomes, the faster the molecules move. As they move around in the liquid, the molecules **collide** with one another. This breaks the intermolecular forces that are holding them together. The molecules rise from the liquid as bubbles of gas and escape into the air. The heat changed liquid molecules into a new state, gas.

Once the water molecules break away from one another, they rise from the water's surface as a gas, as shown in this model.

The steam that rises from this pot of boiling water is water vapor. Over time all the water in this pot will become vaporized.

Every liquid becomes a gas at a different temperature. This temperature is called the liquid's boiling point. The boiling point for water is 212° F (100° C). Once a liquid is heated to its boiling point, it cannot get any hotter. If more heat is added to a boiling liquid, this heat changes the liquid into a gas. It does not make the liquid hotter.

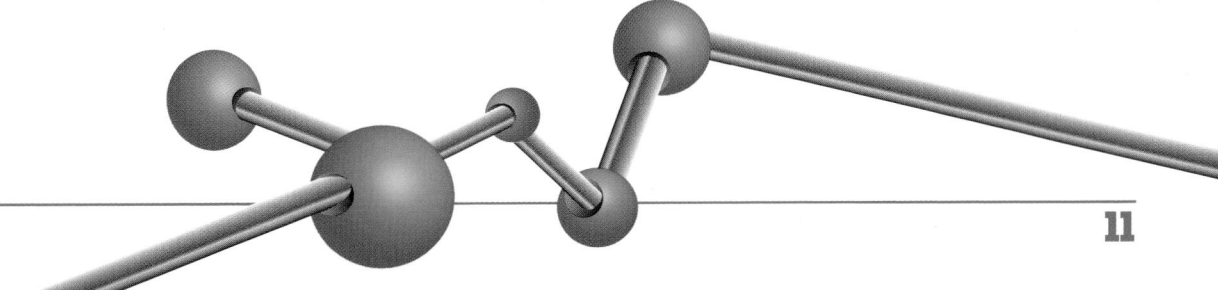

# Evaporation

Have you ever watched someone boil a pot of water to make spaghetti? The steam above the pot is water in the form of a gas. When water turns into a gas and enters the air, this is called evaporation.

Hot water evaporates faster than cold water does. For example, a puddle of water on a sidewalk on a hot, sunny day will evaporate much faster than a puddle on a cool, cloudy day.

The speed at which a liquid evaporates depends on the type of liquid and its temperature. The warmer the liquid, the more energy its molecules have. The more energy a molecule has, the faster it moves. When a fast-moving molecule comes near the surface of a liquid, it can break the bonds holding it in the liquid. The molecule then enters the gaseous state.

The amount of a liquid's surface that is **exposed** to the air also has an effect on evaporation. When a liquid can spread out, more molecules in the liquid have a chance to escape and join other molecules in the air. Suppose you had two cups of water. Would water left in the cup evaporate faster or slower than the same amount of water poured out on a cookie sheet?

Wet clothing dries faster on a clothesline than it does if it is left in a pile. More of the clothing's surface is exposed, so the clothing dries faster.

# Condensation

Sometimes molecules from a liquid that have become a gas turn back into a liquid again. This is called condensation. For example, have you ever noticed that small drops of water form on your window on a cool morning? As air comes in contact with a warmer surface, it can leave tiny drops of water.

Scientists use condensation to separate liquids that have been mixed together. When a **mixture** is heated, the liquid with the lowest boiling point

The drops of water you find on grass in the morning are called dew. Dew is formed when water molecules that evaporated into the air during a hot summer day cool during the night and condense back into water.

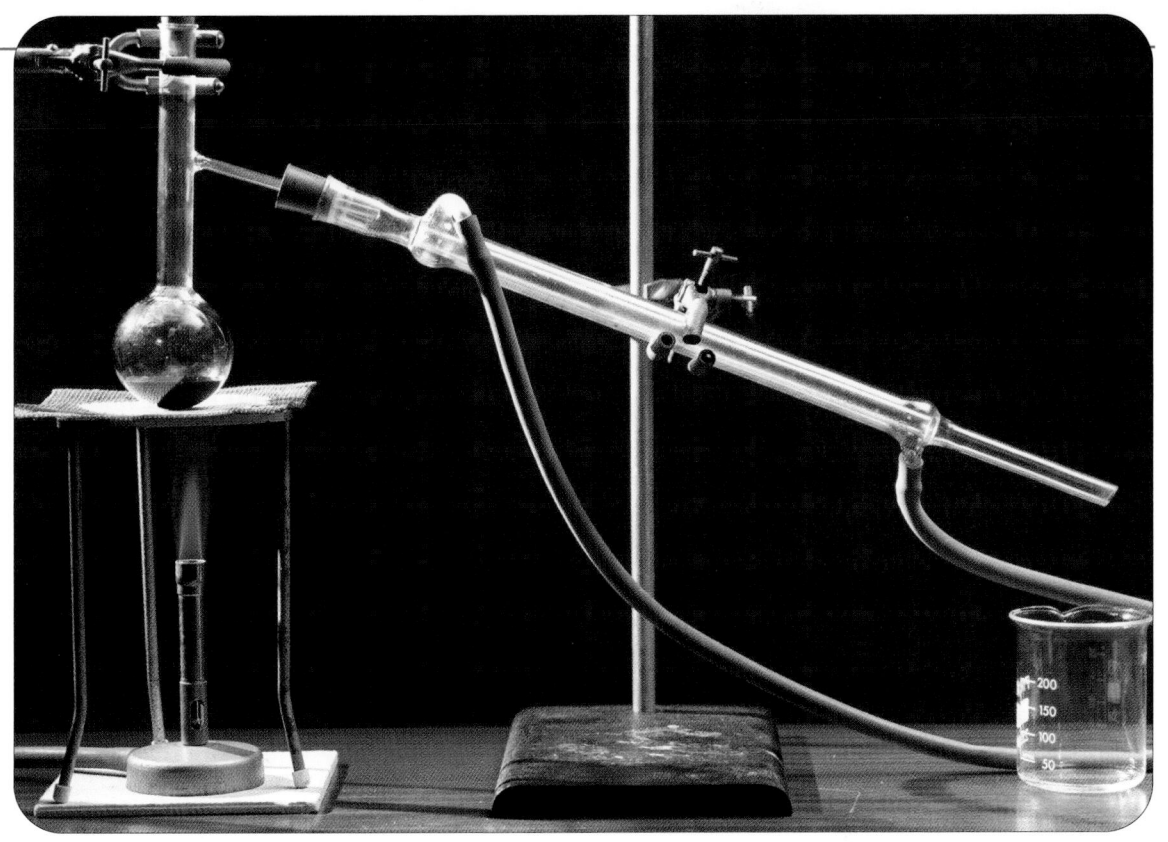

This distillation tool is separating a mixture of water and ink. Water turns into a gas faster than ink does. Once the water has vaporized, only ink will remain in the tube on the left.

will change into a gas first. This gas can be saved in a separate container. When the gas cools, it will condense. The liquid can then be **recovered**. Boiling liquids and condensing their gases is called distillation.

# Liquids in Solutions

A solution is created when matter is dissolved in a liquid. The liquid is called the solvent. The substance being dissolved is the solute. Sometimes solutions are made of two liquids mixed together. For example, when you mix chocolate syrup into milk, you have created a solution of chocolate milk. In a solution made with two liquids, the liquid that you used

Solute

Solvent

the most of is the solvent.

In time the solvent becomes so full of solute that it does not dissolve anymore. When this occurs the solution is saturated. The amount of solute that can be dissolved in a solvent depends on the strength of the intermolecular forces of the solute and the solvent. A solute and a solvent that have the same types of intermolecular forces will easily form a solution. Milk and water have intermolecular forces that are alike. They will form a solution easily. Water and oil are not alike. They will not form a solution easily.

Drop two spoonfuls of ice cream into a glass of milk. Ice cream is the solute, and milk is the solvent.

Solution

# Special Properties of Liquids

Have you ever wondered how bugs walk across the surface of water? Molecules on a liquid's surface are attracted to both the air molecules above them and the liquid molecules below them. The liquid molecules pull harder,

Surface tension keeps this long-legged bug from sinking. This bug is called a water strider. To stride means to take long steps.

causing surface tension. This tension tightens up the top of the water and forms a smooth, skinlike covering. Insects use the covering to move across the water.

Strong forces, or bonds, between molecules give liquid molecules the property of cohesion. Cohesion is the ability to stick together. This is why droplets of liquids form round shapes. The drops are round because the liquid molecules clump together.

Molecules of a liquid are also attracted to the walls of their container. This attraction, known as adhesion, allows a liquid to stick to a solid. Adhesion gives liquids, such as water, the ability to wet paper, wood, or other solids.

Mercury is the only metal that is a liquid at room temperature. Mercury, like all liquids, forms round shapes.

# Liquids and Density

Scientists use the word "density" to describe the amount of matter in a certain volume. Density is how close together the molecules are in a substance. Liquids are usually less dense than solids but more dense than air.

Temperature can change a liquid's density. For example, increasing the temperature of water causes the molecules to spread farther apart. The farther apart the molecules are, the less dense the water

You need to mix oil-and-vinegar dressing before sprinkling it on your salad. Over time the oil floats to the top of the bottle because oil is less dense than vinegar is.

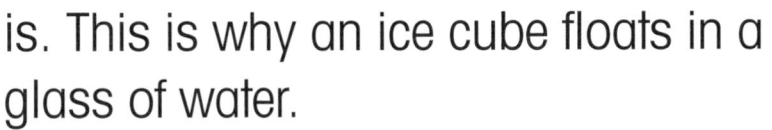

is. This is why an ice cube floats in a glass of water.

The **physical** property of density helps scientists separate liquids. When two liquids are placed in a container, the denser liquid will fall to the bottom. The less dense liquid will rise to the top. This is why oil floats above vinegar in a bottle of salad dressing before it is shaken. Vinegar is a sour liquid used in cooking.

Have you ever seen a lava lamp? As the colored liquid in a lava lamp is heated at the bottom of the lamp, it becomes less dense. The colored liquid then rises to the top and cools, where it becomes slightly more dense. Then it drops to the bottom of the lamp again.

# The Most Important Liquid

Liquids make up most of our world and our bodies. Water is Earth's most important liquid. Rivers, lakes, and oceans cover almost three-quarters of Earth's surface. Our bodies are almost 60 **percent** water by weight. This means that when you step on a scale, water makes up about 60 percent of your weight. Without water people and other living things cannot live.

We now know that most liquids have some physical properties in common. Because water is all around us, we can study its properties to help us understand less familiar liquids. What does water have in common with honey, paint, shampoo, and cooking oil? By observing the liquids around you and comparing their properties, you are thinking like a scientist.

# Glossary

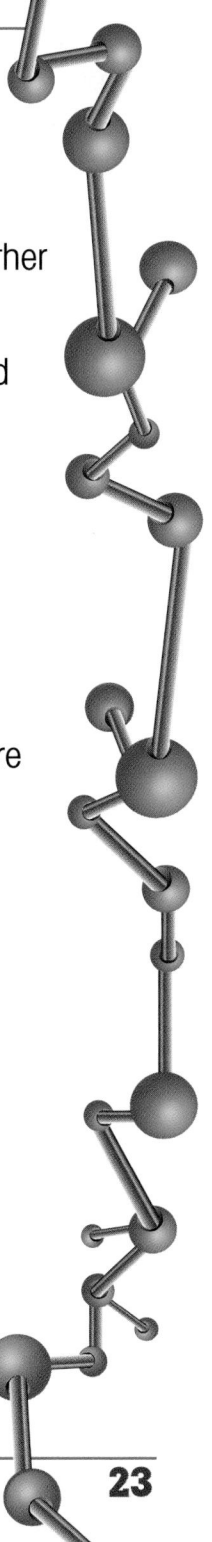

**atoms** (A-temz)  The smallest parts of elements that can exist either alone or with other elements.

**attraction** (uh-TRAK-shun)  Pulling something together or toward something else.

**collide** (kuh-LYD)  To crash together.

**container** (kun-TAY-ner)  Something that holds things.

**energy** (EH-nur-jee)  The power to work or to act.

**exposed** (ik-SPOHZD)  Not covered.

**mixture** (MIKS-cher)  A new thing that is made when two or more things are mixed together.

**percent** (pur-SENT)  One part of 100.

**physical** (FIH-zih-kul)  Having to do with natural forces.

**recovered** (rih-KUH-verd)  Got back.

**substance** (SUB-stans)  Any matter that takes up space.

**temperature** (TEM-pur-cher)  How hot or cold something is.

# Index

**A**
adhesion, 19
atoms, 4
attraction, 5

**B**
boiling point, 11

**C**
condensation,
    14–15

**D**
density, 20–21

**E**
energy, 10, 12
evaporation, 12–13

**F**
freezing point, 18

**G**
gas(es), 4, 14–15

**I**
intermolecular forces,
    5, 17

**M**
melting point, 8
mixture, 15

**S**
solid, 4
solute, 16–17
solution, 16–17
solvent, 16–17
surface tension, 19

# Web Sites

Due to the changing nature of Internet links, PowerKids Press has developed an online list of Web sites related to the subject of this book. This site is updated regularly. Please use this link to access the list:

www.powerkidslinks.com/lops/liquids/